WAR MACHINES
AEROPLANES

Simon Adams

FRANKLIN WATTS
LONDON•SYDNEY

IN ASSOCIATION WITH

IMPERIAL WAR
MUSEUM

First published in 2007 by Franklin Watts

Franklin Watts
338 Euston Road
London NW1 3BH

Franklin Watts Australia
Level 17/207 Kent Street
Sydney, NSW 2000

A CIP catalogue record for this book is available
from the British Library.

Dewey number: 623.7'46

ISBN 978 0 7496 7168 6

Printed in China

Franklin Watts is a division of Hachette Children's
Books, an Hachette Livre UK company.

Editor: Sarah Ridley
Editor-in-chief: John C. Miles
Designer: Jason Billin
Art director: Jonathan Hair

Picture credits
Cover main Wikimedia Commons: Chowells

All other images copyright © Imperial War Museum. Cover bottom left ZZZ4727E, bottom middle
Q63847, bottom right NYP65472;Title page Q67902; page 4 Q63847; page 5 CH2926; page 6
Q68124; page 7 Q57615A; page 8 Q67902; page 9 Q20641; page 10 Q63786; page 11 Q63784;
page 12 Q63847; page 13 top Q44797, bottom Q50329; page 14 Q63778; page 15 Q63779;
page 16 Q67573; page 17 Q67328; page 18 HU44156; page 19 MH6665; page 20 EA74532;
page 21 top AP12412, bottom EA19178; page 22 CH2926; page 23 CH5249; page 24 OEM
3647; page 25 ZZZ5806E; page 26 CH6299; page 27 left NYP65472, right EH18955; page 28
HU95885; HU95886; page 30 background Q63779.

389.2

T22578

This book is due for return on or before the last date shown below.

Contents

Introduction

On 17 December 1903, the Wright brothers took to the skies in their aircraft 'Flyer' at Kitty Hawk in North Carolina, USA. Their short flight was the first controlled, powered aircraft flight in human history.

The First World War

Early aircraft were small, flimsy machines, carrying only the pilot and perhaps one crew. But a little over ten years later, in 1914, the First World War broke out in Europe. Aircraft now became weapons of war. The fighters were equipped with machine guns to attack each other in the skies, while some larger aircraft had enough space to carry bombs to drop on enemy territory. By the end of the war in 1918, aircraft were large and powerful enough to fly much longer distances.

The Second World War

Twenty years later, in 1939, the Second World War broke out. The new fighter aircraft were small and fast, while massive, slow-moving bombers carried a vast weight of bombs to rain down on enemy towns and cities.

All 12 aircraft in this book flew during these two world wars. Each one has an interesting story to tell, and all of them show how rapidly aircraft developed from that first day in North Carolina when powered flight began.

ROYAL AIRCRAFT FACTORY
BE2c

The Royal Aircraft Factory BE2c first flew in February 1912 and entered war service in 1914 as a reconnaissance (observation) aircraft.

However, it was slow and hard to manoeuvre, making it an easy target for German fighter planes. From 1917 onwards, a later version was used only for home defence and to train new pilots.

Airship shot down

The BE2 did have one moment of fame when, on the night of 2/3 September 1916, it shot down the first German airship over Britain. The pilot, Captain William Leefe Robinson, was awarded the Victoria Cross for his brave attack on the airship.

▼ *The BE2c was a flimsy, underpowered aeroplane and was easily attacked by German fighters.*

FACT FILE

★ The BE stands for Blériot Experimental, named after Louis Blériot, the French pilot who made the first flight across the English Channel on 25 July 1909.

★ The second crew member, the observer, was armed only with a rifle in the first models of the BE2. In the BE2c a machine gun was provided for his use.

PERFORMANCE

Maximum speed	120 km/h (75 mph)
Range	320 km (200 miles)
Service ceiling	3,048 m (10,000 ft)

▼ *A biplane has two parallel wings, usually supported by solid struts and wire rope.*

SPECS & STATS

Crew	2 – pilot and observer	**Span**	11.28 m (37 ft)
Height	3.4 m (11 ft 1 in)	**Length**	8.31 m (27 ft 3 in)
Loaded weight	972 kg (2,142 lb)		
Armaments	1 x 7.7 mm (0.303 in) Lewis machine gun		
	2 x 51 kg (112 lb) or 10 x 9 kg (20 lb) bombs		
Engine	1 x Royal Aircraft Factory 1a, 90 hp engine		

SOPWITH CAMEL F.1

The Sopwith Camel was one of the main British fighter planes during the later years of the First World War.

The Camel first flew in December 1916. More than 5,500 were produced before the war ended in November 1918.

A challenge to fly

The Camel could make some clever moves but was not easy to fly. Engine, pilot, guns and fuel tank were all placed in the first 2 m (7 ft) of the aircraft, which made it difficult to handle. In addition, the Clerget engine needed exactly the right fuel mixture or else it choked and cut out during take-off. Despite these problems, the Camel was successful in combat, shooting down 1,294 German aircraft.

▼ *The short, stubby Camel.*

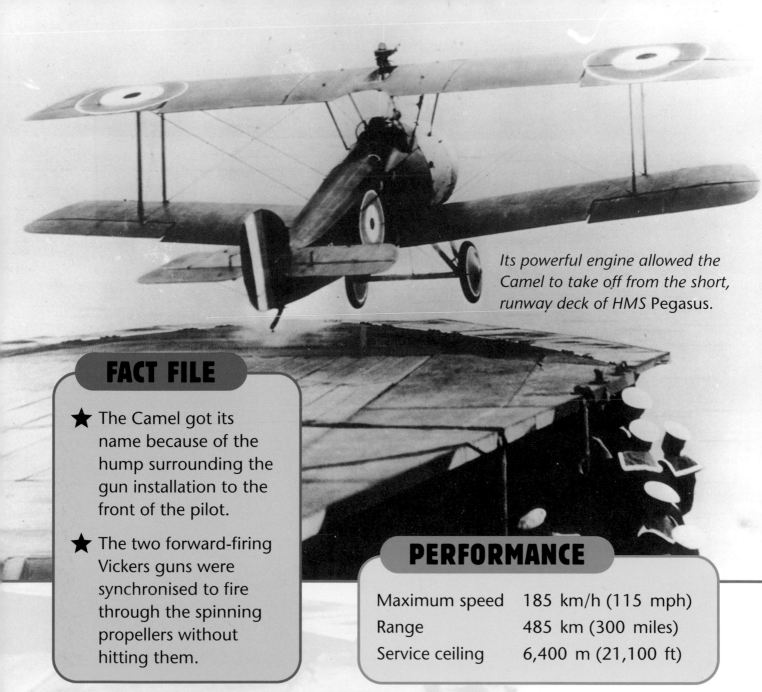

Its powerful engine allowed the Camel to take off from the short, runway deck of HMS Pegasus.

FACT FILE

★ The Camel got its name because of the hump surrounding the gun installation to the front of the pilot.

★ The two forward-firing Vickers guns were synchronised to fire through the spinning propellers without hitting them.

PERFORMANCE

Maximum speed	185 km/h (115 mph)
Range	485 km (300 miles)
Service ceiling	6,400 m (21,100 ft)

SPECS & STATS

Crew	1 – pilot	**Span**	8.53 m (28 ft 0 in)
Height	2.59 m (8 ft 6 in)	**Length**	5.71 m (18 ft 9 in)
Loaded weight	660 kg (1,455 lb)		
Armaments	2 x 7.7 mm (0.303 in) Vickers machine guns		
Engine	1 x Clerget 9B, 9-cylinder, 130 hp rotary engine		

Gotha G.V

▼ *The Gotha G.V was an extremely effective bomber.*

The Gotha G.V was the fifth in a series of heavy bombers used by the German air service during the First World War.

The Germans first used vast Zeppelin airships to drop bombs on London and other targets in south-east England. However, the airships were too slow and easy to hit, and so were replaced in summer 1917 by the Gotha bombers.

FACT FILE

★ The Gotha began life as a large, twin-engine seaplane that was adapted to become a land-based bomber by its designer, Oskar Ursinus, when he was conscripted into the German army in 1914.

★ An opening in the underside of the fuselage allowed the rear gunner to fire at targets below and behind the bomber.

Royal Air Force begins

The Gotha bombers caused huge alarm, as the British had few aircraft in 1917 able to catch the Gothas and prevent them from attacking. The British therefore reorganised their air defences, creating the Royal Air Force, the world's first independent air force, by about January 1918.

▼ *Its 23.7-m (77 ft 9 in) wingspan made the Gotha G.V instantly recognisable from the ground.*

PERFORMANCE

Maximum speed	140 km/h (87 mph)
Range	840 km (520 miles)
Service ceiling	6,500 m (21,300 ft)

SPECS & STATS

Crew	3 – pilot, gunner and bomber, rear gunner
Span	23.7 m (77 ft 9 in) **Height** 4.5 m (14 ft)
Length	12.42 m (40 ft 9 in)
Loaded weight	3,967 kg (8,745 lb)
Armaments	2 or 3 x 7.92 mm (0.312 in) Parabellum LMG 14 machine guns 500 kg (1,102 lb) bombs
Engines	2 x Mercedes D.IVa inline, 260 hp engines

Fokker
Dr.1 Triplane

The German Fokker triplane made its appearance over the battlefields of Western Europe in August 1917.

The new aircraft was very manoeuvrable but it was much slower than many of the Allies' fighter planes and difficult to land.

The 'Red Baron'

The most famous pilot to fly a Fokker Dr.1 was Baron Manfred von Richthofen, the 'Red Baron'. The legendary air ace made his name when he painted his Albatros D.111 fighter bright red. He shot down perhaps 80 enemy aircraft before he himself was shot down and killed on 21 April 1918.

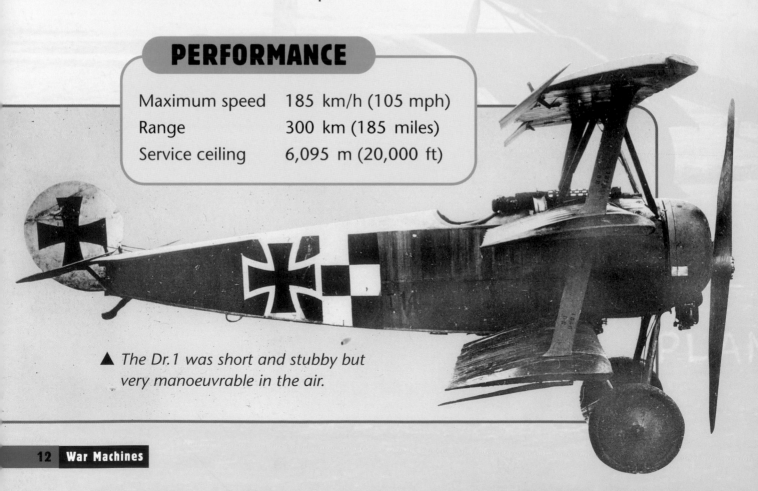

PERFORMANCE

Maximum speed	185 km/h (105 mph)
Range	300 km (185 miles)
Service ceiling	6,095 m (20,000 ft)

▲ *The Dr.1 was short and stubby but very manoeuvrable in the air.*

FACT FILE

★ The Dr. in the title stands for *Dreidecker*, the German word for a triplane.

★ The photo on the right shows part of the wall in von Richthofen's quarters. Displayed are numbers taken from enemy aircraft shot down by him.

The Germans often painted faces on the front of their aeroplanes.

SPECS & STATS

Crew 1 – pilot	**Span** 7.2 m (23 ft 7 in)
Height 2.95 m (9 ft 8 in)	**Length** 5.77 m (18 ft 11 in)

Loaded weight 586 kg (1,292 lb)

Armaments 2 x 7.92 mm (0.312 in) LMG 08/15 Spandau machine guns

Engine 1 x Oberursel UR.II, 9-cylinder, 110 hp rotary engine

Fokker D.VII

The German Fokker D.VII fighter only made its appearance at the very end of the First World War, but it quickly proved to be the best fighter in the sky.

It could dive and climb with ease and easily outmanoeuvred many enemy aircraft.

Fearsome fighter

Indeed, the Fokker was so feared by Britain and France that it was the only aircraft to be mentioned in the armistice (ceasefire) agreements that ended the war with Germany in November 1918: the Germans were told to 'surrender in good condition … all aircraft of the D.VII type.'

▼ *The crosses on the fuselage, tail and wings identify this as a German aeroplane.*

FOKKER BIPLANE.

▼ *The Fokker D.VII was easily the best fighter of the war.*

PERFORMANCE

Maximum speed	186 km/h (116 mph)
Range	2 m (170 miles)
Service ceiling	5,970 m (19,600 ft)

FACT FILE

★ Many D.VIIs were covered with linen printed in irregular coloured shapes. These shapes merged together at a distance to form an effective camouflage.

★ The use of printed fabric rather than paint reduced the body weight of the aircraft.

SPECS & STATS

Crew	1 – pilot	**Span**	8.93 m (29 ft 3 in)
Height	2.8 m (9 ft 2 in)	**Length**	6.93 m (22 ft 9 in)
Loaded weight	850 kg (1,874 lb)		
Armaments	2 x 7.92 mm (0.312 in) LMG 08/15 Spandau machine guns		
Engine	1 x Mercedes D111a, 180 hp engine		

Vickers
Vimy FB 27A

The Vickers Vimy entered service in October 1918, at the very end of the First World War, and so played no part in the conflict.

However, it served successfully as the main heavy bomber of the Royal Air Force throughout the 1920s.

Trans-Atlantic first

The aircraft does have one massive claim to fame, however. In June 1919 Captain John Alcock and Lieutenant Arthur Brown flew a modified Vickers Vimy non-stop across the Atlantic Ocean from Newfoundland in Canada to Connemara in Ireland, the first time this had been achieved. The aircraft flew through so much snow and ice that Brown had to continually climb onto the wings to remove ice from the engines' air intakes.

▼ *The Vickers Vimy was an effective bomber and a good long-distance aircraft.*

PERFORMANCE

Maximum speed	165 km/h (100 mph)
Range	1,448 km (900 miles)
Service ceiling	2,135 m (7,000 ft)

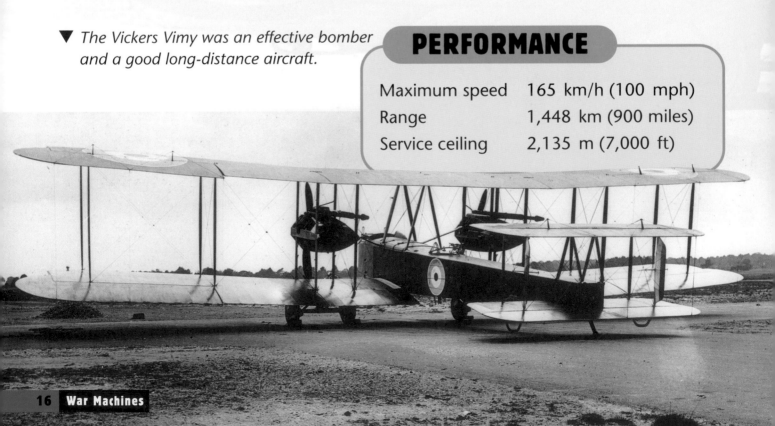

FACT FILE

★ The first Vickers Vimy flew on 30 November 1917. It was named after the Battle of Vimy Ridge, during which Canadian troops captured the ridge in eastern France from the Germans in April 1917.

★ The Vimy was a very versatile aircraft. Versions were made for civilian use, to transport military equipment and as an air ambulance to carry wounded servicemen to hospital.

▲ *Early versions of the Vickers Vimy had Fiat rather than Rolls-Royce engines.*

SPECS & STATS

Crew	3 – pilot, front gunner and bomb-aimer, rear gunner
Span	20.75 m (68 ft 1 in) **Height** 4.76 m (15 ft 8 in)
Length	13.27 m (43 ft 7 in)
Loaded weight	4,937 kg (10,884 lb)
Armaments	2 x 7.7 mm (0.303 in) Lewis machine guns 1,123 kg (2,476 lb) bombs
Engines	2 x Rolls-Royce Eagle VIII, 360 hp engines

Messerschmitt Bf 109E

The Messerschmitt Bf 109E was one of the first modern fighters of the Second World War. It included such features as a closed canopy and retractable landing gear.

It also used the revolutionary new monocoque construction that did away with internal frameworks and carried the weight of the plane in its all-metal skin.

Germany's workhorse

The Bf 109E was the standard fighter of the Luftwaffe in the Second World War. It also served as an escort fighter, interceptor, ground-attack and reconnaissance aircraft. It made its maiden flight on 28 May 1935. More than 31,000 were built before the end of the Second World War, more than any other fighter aircraft in history.

▼ *The retractable wheels helped to make the Messerschmitt aerodynamic in flight.*

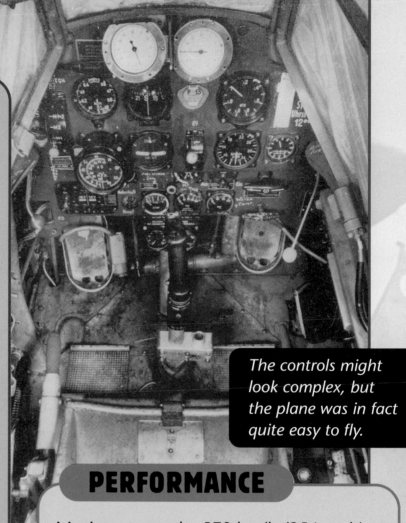

FACT FILE

★ The 'Bf' of the aircraft's title referred to the Bayerische Flugzeuwerke (Bavarian Aircraft Works) company that designed the aircraft. When the chief designer, Willy Messerschmitt, took over the company and renamed it in 1938, the aircraft became known as the Me 109, although the old name remained in frequent use.

★ The 'E' of its title stood for Emil, as all the early Messerschmitt Bf models had personal names – A for Anton, B for Bruno, C for Caesar, D for Dora and so on.

The controls might look complex, but the plane was in fact quite easy to fly.

PERFORMANCE

Maximum speed	570 km/h (354 mph) at 6,300 m (20,677 ft)
Range	663 km (412 miles)
Service ceiling	11,000 m (36,091 ft)

SPECS & STATS

Crew	1 – pilot
Height	3.4 m (11 ft 2 in)
Span	9.85 m (32 ft 4 in)
Length	8.63 m (28 ft 4 in)
Loaded weight	2,505 kg (5,523 lb)
Armaments	2 x 7.92 mm (0.312 in) MG 17 machine guns above the engine 2 x MG FF/M cannons in the wings
Engine	1 x Daimler-Benz DB 601A–1, liquid-cooled, inverted V–12, 1,100 hp engine

Boeing B-17G
Flying Fortress

▲ *Many Flying Fortresses were left unpainted.*

The American Boeing B-17 'Flying Fortress' is one of the most famous aircraft ever built. The B-17 prototype first flew on 28 July 1935.

A journalist on the *Seattle Times* saw the plane and nicknamed it the 'Flying Fortress' because it had so many guns. Boeing quickly saw the value of this new name and trademarked it for use.

The aircraft served in every Second World War combat zone, but is best known for the daylight bombing of Germany. Production ended in May 1945 and totalled 12,731.

PERFORMANCE

Maximum speed	462 km/h (287 mph)
Cruising speed	293 km/h (182 mph)
Range	3,219 km (2,000 miles)
Service ceiling	10,850 m (35,600 ft)

▶ Armoured 'flak jackets' saved the lives of many gun-turret crew members.

SPECS & STATS

Crew	10 – pilot, co-pilot, navigator, bombardier/ nose-gunner, flight-engineer/top-turret gunner, radio operator, 2 waist gunners, ball-turret gunner, tail gunner
Span	31.62 m (103 ft 9 in)
Height	5.82 m (19 ft 1 in)
Length	22.66 m (74 ft 4 in)
Loaded weight	32,659 kg (72,000 lb)
Armaments	13 x 12.7 mm (0.50 in) M2 Browning machine guns 3,600 kg (8,000 lb) bombs on short-range missions – up to 640 km (400 miles) 2,000 kg (4,500 lb) bombs on long-range missions – up to 1,280 km (800 miles)
Engines	4 x Wright R-1820-97 Cyclone, turbo-supercharged, radial 1,200 hp engines

FACT FILE

★ The ball-turret gunner had to stay in position throughout a flight – no rest stops for him!

★ The B–17 flew during daylight and was open to enemy attack – it needed an escort of fighter planes.

US servicemen load a bomb on a B-17 they hope will make a direct hit.

SPECIAL EASTER EGG FOR "HITLER"

Supermarine Spitfire

The British single-seater Spitfire was probably the most famous fighter of all during the Second World War.

It was also the only fighter that was in continual production before, during and after the war.

The Battle of Britain

In 1940, when Britain was under attack from the German Luftwaffe, Spitfire pilots took to the skies every day to protect Britain from aerial attack. They attempted to prevent the German bombers from getting through to drop their bombs on British ports and airfields. To many people at the time, the Spitfire pilots were the heroes of what was known as the 'Battle of Britain'.

A Spitfire in flight over the green fields of southern England.

FACT FILE

★ The word 'spitfire' dates from the reign of Elizabeth I (1558–1603) and refers to a fiery, ferocious type of person, usually a woman. The chief designer of the aircraft, R J Mitchell, was not impressed, stating that it was the 'sort of silly name they would give it.'

★ There were 24 different types of Spitfire produced, as well as many variations of those types. The most common was the Mk V, with 6,479 built. In total, 22,789 Spitfires took to the skies between 1938 and 1948, when production ended.

PERFORMANCE

Maximum speed	582 km/h (362 mph)
Range	636 km (395 miles)
Service ceiling	9,723 m (31,900 ft)

▲ *The shape of the Spitfire's wingtips made it instantly recognisable.*

SPECS & STATS

Crew	1 – pilot	**Span**	11.2 m (36 ft 10 in)
Height	3.5 m (11 ft 5 in)	**Length**	9.1 m (29 ft 11 in)
Loaded weight	2,624 kg (5,784 lb)		
Armaments	8 x 7.7 mm (0.303 in) Browning machine guns		
Engine	1 x Rolls-Royce Merlin III, 1,030 hp engine		

Douglas SBD Dauntless

The Douglas SBD Dauntless was the US navy's main dive bomber in the early years of the war in the Pacific Ocean against Japan.

It was involved in the Pacific War from the start when the Japanese attacked Dauntlesses from USS *Enterprise* at Pearl Harbor on 7 December 1941.

The Battle of Midway

The most important contribution made by the Dauntless occurred at the Battle of Midway in June 1942. Operating from aircraft carriers and escorted by F4F Wildcat fighters, Dauntlesses sank four Japanese aircraft carriers and heavily damaged two cruisers.

Four Dauntlesses cruise over the Pacific during the Second World War.

► *A pair of Dauntlesses prepare for action on the deck of a US aircraft carrier.*

FACT FILE

★ A dive bomber dives straight down at its target at high speed and releases its bombs as close to the target as possible. In this way, it avoids some anti-aircraft fire and can accurately place its bombs on a relatively small or moving target.

★ From its first delivery in May 1940, 5,936 aircraft were produced until the last one was manufactured on 21 July 1944.

PERFORMANCE

Maximum speed	410 km/h (255 mph)
Range	1,244 km (773 miles)
Service ceiling	7,780 m (25,530 ft)

SPECS & STATS

Crew 2 – pilot, gunner   **Span** 12.65 m (41 ft 6 in)

Height 4.14 m (13 ft 7 in)   **Length** 10.08 m (33 ft 1 in)

Loaded weight 4,843 kg (10,676 lb)

Armaments 2 x 12.7 mm (0.5 in) forward-firing machine guns
2 x 7.62 mm (0.3 in) flexible-mounted machine guns
1,020 kg (2,250 lb) bombs

Engine 1 x Wright R-1820-60, radial 1,200 hp engine

Mustang
P-51

The North American Mustang P–51 entered military service in 1942 and soon became one of the most successful aircraft in the Second World War.

The Mustang was a single-seat fighter aircraft and was used to escort bombers when they raided Germany. It also saw service against the Japanese in the Pacific.

The maiden flight of the Mustang took place on 26 October 1940. Although mainly used as a fighter, it was possible to increase its bomb-carrying capacity and turn the aircraft into a useful fighter-bomber.

▼ *Here shown with RAF insignia, the P-51 Mustang was one of the most versatile aircraft of the Second World War.*

FACT FILE

★ The teardrop-shaped bubble canopy on later models (right) gave the pilot unrestricted vision in all directions.

★ After the war, many Mustangs were converted for civilian use and were particularly well suited for air racing.

SPECS & STATS

Crew   1 – pilot   **Span**   11.28 m (37 ft)

Height 4.17 m (13 ft 8 in)   **Length** 9.83 m (32 ft 3 in)

Loaded weight   4,175 kg (9,200 lb)

Armaments   6 x 12.77 mm (0.5 in) machine guns; 400 rounds per gun
for the two inboard guns, 270 rounds per outboard gun
10 x 127 mm (5 in) rockets
907 kg (2,000 lb) bombs

Engine   1 x Packard Merlin V-1650-7, liquid-cooled, supercharged,
V-12, 1,695 hp engine

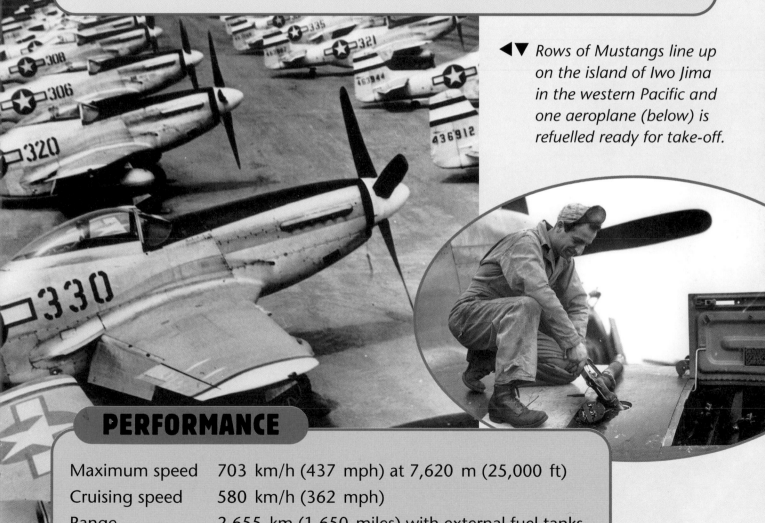

◀▼ *Rows of Mustangs line up
on the island of Iwo Jima
in the western Pacific and
one aeroplane (below) is
refuelled ready for take-off.*

PERFORMANCE

Maximum speed   703 km/h (437 mph) at 7,620 m (25,000 ft)

Cruising speed   580 km/h (362 mph)

Range   2,655 km (1,650 miles) with external fuel tanks

Service ceiling   12,770 m (41,900 ft)

Avro
Lancaster

On the night of 17 May 1943, a group of Avro Lancaster bombers from 617 Squadron carried out the 'dambusters' raid, one of the most famous air raids of the Second World War.

The dambusters

The aircraft dropped specially designed bouncing bombs that skimmed across reservoirs before sinking to explode at the base of their targets – the Eder and Möhne dams in the Ruhr valley of Germany. The dams collapsed, sending walls of water through the Ruhr valley and flooding many mines and factories.

▼ The Avro Lancaster could carry a vast weight of bombs.

The Lancaster was designed as a night bomber, although it was also used for daytime bombing and reconnaissance work. Its 10.05-m (33-ft) long bomb bay allowed it to carry bombs as heavy as 9,980 kg (22,000 lbs).

▲ *The undercarriage needed to be sturdy to support the Lancaster when it landed after a bombing mission.*

FACT FILE

★ The Avro Lancaster made its maiden flight on 9 January 1941 and was introduced into Royal Air Force service the following year. A total of 7,377 aircraft were produced.

★ Lancasters flew 156,000 operations and dropped 608,612 tons of bombs from 1942 to 1945.

PERFORMANCE

Maximum speed	450 km/h (280 mph) at 5,600 m (15,000 ft)
Cruising speed	322 km/h (200 mph)
Range	4,300 km (2,700 miles) with minimal bomb load
Service ceiling	8,160 m (23,500 ft)

SPECS & STATS

Crew	7 – pilot, flight engineer, navigator, bomb aimer, wireless operator, mid-upper gunner, rear gunner
Span	31.09 m (102 ft)
Length	21.18 m (69 ft 5 in)
Height	5.97 m (19 ft 7 in)
Loaded weight	29,000 kg (63,000 lb)
Armaments	8 x 7.7 mm (0.303 in) Browning machine guns in three turrets 10,000 kg (22,000 lb) bombs, maximum
Engines	4 x Rolls-Royce Merlin XX, V-12 1,280 hp engines

Glossary

Biplane
Aircraft with two parallel wings, one on top of the other.

Bomber
Aircraft designed to carry and drop bombs.

Camouflage
Use of paint, material or other substance to conceal the outlines of an aircraft and thus confuse the enemy.

Canopy
Glass and metal cover above the cockpit to protect the pilot.

Dive bomber
Aircraft that dives almost vertically to attack its target.

Escort plane
An aircraft accompanying another in order to protect it from enemy attack.

Fighter
Aircraft designed to fight other aircraft.

Fuselage
Main body of an aircraft.

hp
Horsepower, a unit of power.

Inline engine
Engine in which the cylinders are in either a single front-to-back row, or in several rows in a 'V' or 'W' shape.

Interceptor
Aircraft designed to attack or prevent an enemy aircraft reaching its target.

Landing gear
Wheels, shock absorbers, struts and other items that support an aircraft on the ground and enable it to take off and land; also called the undercarriage.

Luftwaffe
The German air force.

Machine gun
Rapid-firing weapon.

Maiden flight
The first-ever flight of an aircraft.

Mk
Short for Mark, the model or type of aircraft.

Monocoque
From the French words *mono* for single and *coque* for eggshell, a construction technique that supports the structural load of the aircraft using its external skin, rather than an internal framework.

Radial engine
Type of aero engine with the cylinders arranged in one or two circular rows around the crankshaft.

Reconnaissance
Obtaining information about the position, activities, resources and intentions of the enemy.

Seaplane
Aircraft that can take off and land on water using floats rather than wheels.

Service ceiling
The highest an aircraft can safely fly without endangering plane or crew.

Trademark
The legally registered name or symbol of a product that is protected by law against competitors.

Triplane
Aircraft with three parallel wings on top of each other.

Victoria Cross
British military award for outstanding bravery, first awarded by Queen Victoria in 1856.

Some useful websites

Wikipedia entries for all the aircraft in this book. Type in the name of the aircraft in the Search box and press Go:
http://en.wikipedia.org/wiki/Main_Page

The Imperial War Museum's official website:
www.iwm.org.uk/

Encyclopedic sites about the two world wars:
www.spartacus.schoolnet.co.uk/FWW.htm
www.spartacus.schoolnet.co.uk/2WW.htm

BBC history sites about the two world wars:
www.bbc.co.uk/history/worldwars/wwone/
www.bbc.co.uk/history/worldwars/wwtwo/

Note to parents and teachers:
Every effort has been made by the Publishers to ensure that the websites in this book are suitable for children, that they are of the highest educational value, and that they contain no inappropriate or offensive material. However, because of the nature of the Internet, it is impossible to guarantee that the contents of these sites will not be altered. We strongly advise that Internet access is supervised by a responsible adult.

Index